I NEED A HUG

By Bil Keane

FAWCETT GOLD MEDAL • NEW YORK

I NEED A HUG

Published by Fawcett Gold Medal Books,
a unit of CBS Publications,
the Consumer Publishing Division of CBS Inc.,
by arrangement with The Register and Tribune Syndicate.

ISBN: 0-449-14147-0

Printed in the United States of America

28   27   26   25   24

"Why do we have to wait till after dinner to tell Daddy
what happened to the car?"

"Can we have a cookout?"

"Look, Mommy! I gave my dolly a new hair-do!"

"It was only a sonic boom!"

"You're sposed to take the one nearest you."

"I don't have my play money any more. I put it in the collection basket."

"DON'T TOUCH! We might not buy this one!"

"Grandma, we're not allowed to ask you for anything but if you give us something we can take it."

"He's listening for germs."

"I thought you told Daddy that PJ was putting EVERY-
THING in his mouth these days."

"Just a minute, Tess..."

"Guess maybe we should have let Mommy help us."

"Okay, now what comes after 10, Mommy."

"You can open your eyes now, Daddy—
the ugly monster's gone."

"We were just drying our hands!"

"Why do you ask for it in a doggy bag when it's for our lunch?"

"I hear my ears ringing. Do you?"

"Is George Washington the one with the ponytail?"

"Mommy and Daddy are NOT senior citizens.
Just Daddy is."

"Why do we call her our GREAT aunt? Did she do something special?"

"We'll call this our DINNER, won't we, Mommy?"

"Mommy, may I have a doughnut?"

"Mommy! PJ's cleaning out the bookcase again! Shall I hit
him for you?"

"When I tell the time I don't know my befores or afters, but I know my o'clocks."

"Mommy isn't hurting Teddy—she's just mending
him for you."

"I have to close this gate so I won't get out."

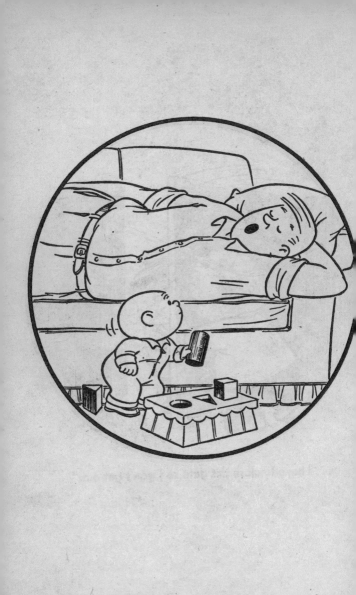

"Just wait 'til I'm a teen-ager! I'll get to babysit you and tell YOU what to do!"

"But picking up my toys isn't anything. I want
to HELP you!"

"Yes, that's Jeffy when he was three months old."

"Why don't you dance with the mop like the lady on TV?"

"Mommy, feel my loose tooth."

"Up, Barfy!"

"Gee, Mommy! PJ and I are playing Hide and Seek
and I can't find him ANYWHERE!"

"Which flavor do you want---red, green, yellow, or purple?
Mine's the red one."

"I put that away for you."

"Wow! I bet he's good at licking pans."

"But, how could goin' outside in her bare FEET give Dolly a cold in her HEAD?"

"Later? When's later?"

"But we didn't open it like that—Daddy did."

"The one thing you have to remember about secrets
is to tell them right into a person's ear."

"Instead of going for a ride, I think I'll stay home and keep Mommy company."

"Why does Daddy have so much homework?
Was he naughty at work?"

"Poor Mommy—when she was little, she had to cut
out her dolls with scissors."

"Won't your knees catch cold?"

"Shall I get this kind Mommy? It's only FIVE CENTS!"

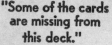

"Some of the cards
are missing from
this deck."

"Mommy! Can you come here quick and tie my shoe?"

"Why don't you ever put the car in the garage, Daddy?"

"Can I still live with you when I get big
and you're my grandma?"

"Bet 'cha Daddy's going to get it when he comes home."

"Could I have some of that left over
pasghetti for breakfast?"

"Can you help me lift this towel, Mommy? I couldn't find a washcloth."

"I've been in the hospital three times. Once to get my ashed finger fixed, once to get stitches in my head, and once to get borned."

"Raisins ARE SO dead grapes, aren't they, Mommy?"

"hose two friends of Daddy's get me all mixed up 'cause
they both have 'Mr.' in their names."

"I know it's his balloon, but my air is in it!"

"He dropped his teddy bear and he wants you to kiss it."

"Children, please! Granddad and Grandma aren't eve
in the HOUSE!"

"Here's your handbag,
Grandma, in case you
want something out of it."

"Grandma's REALLY mad this time—when she called Mommy she said 'Thel' instead of 'Mommy'!"

"We wish you weren't going home, Grandma. While you're here Mommy just scolds us in whispers."

"How come when PJ sticks out his tongue, it's cute, but if we did it, we'd get spanked?"

"No, no . . . you must always shake hands with the RIGHT hand."

"Daddy said those pictures he took when Grandma was here were still in the camera, but we can't find them."

"When I grow up I'm going to be a lion tamer—if
Mommy will come in the cage with me."

"I see you had some help loading the grocery cart."

"You can try some of mine, Mr. Clark, but Mommy will make
you go out in the backyard to use it."

"What else does your husband like to play with besides his home barber's kit?"

"While we were out for a ride we stopped in to see
Grandma for a minute."

"No buying ice cream or candy for Jeffy while you're out—
it'd spoil his dinner."

"What'll it be? A peanut butter sandwich with two bites out of it; what's left of a dish of fruit cocktail with the cherries missing; half a jar of cereal, egg yolk and bacon..."

"MOMMY! Open up!
MOMMY! MOMMY!"

"May we have a drink
of water?"

"I offered to kiss it, but he preferred treatment by a specialist."

"Why does the sun go to bed later than I do these days?"

"Pulling at the flowers is a no-no, playing in the street is a no-no, eating dirt is a no-no..."

"Only 208 days till Christmas!"

"We're going to have a funeral! Jeffy ran over a cricket with his bike."

"It's ONLY for a couple of weeks!"

"Do I have time to get a drink of water before we leave?"

"I'm telling! Your foot's wet—you didn't wait an hour after eating!"

"It's a heartbreaking way to learn about tides."

"They're kissing again!"

"No more...this is enough...hold it....this is a FINE collection...no more..."

"Don't you think grandma would like this one better?"

"I hope it NEVER stops raining!"

"Can't we stay just one more day?"

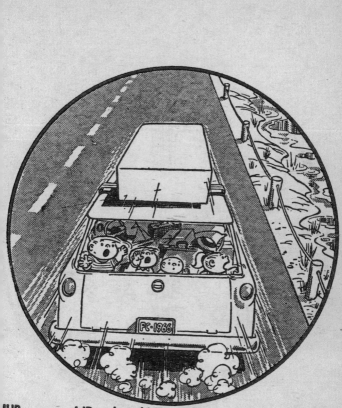

"'Bye, ocean! 'Bye, beach! 'Bye, sand castles! 'Bye, board-walk! 'Bye, sea gulls! 'Bye, pizza palace! 'Bye, boats! 'Bye, merry-go-round!..."

"Couldn't you just GIVE them their postcards when we get home?"

"No, Love, vacation's over. You'll have to get used to Daddy
going out without you."

"If you and Daddy ever get a new baby, will you make sure it's a girl?"

"The ants were bothering me."

"Grandma's on the phone! She wants to buy a quarter's worth, and we can drink it for her!"

"Can we stop for an ice cream cone?"

"The part of golf I like best is walking in the woods!"

"Quick, everybody! The sun's setting right in that field! Let's go qet it!"

"Miss McElfresh says we're supposed to have a five-point
breakfast every morning—fruit, cereal, toast, egg, milk..."

"We'll be right back after we watch 'Captain Kangaroo!'"

"Are you sure they're BOYS' boots? They look like the ones Dolly wore last year!"

"I learned how to read TWO SENTENCES today. One is
'David.' The other is 'David, come!'"

"Know what next Wednesday is, Daddy? It's your birthday but we're not giving you a surprise party or anything like that."

"Wednesday's our Daddy's birthday and we're giving him a SURPRISE PARTY!"

"SURPRISE!" "Can you cut the cake now, Daddy?"

"We don't have enough leaves in our yard so we're bring-
ing some over from the Mosby's!"

"I wanted to carry in the cookies!"

"What happens if we say 'Trick or Treat' and somebody says 'Trick'?"

"I want YOU two to bring me YOUR bags of Halloween candy
at once!"

"Do you want to catch cold, young man? How many times have I told you not to run around without your slippers?"

"A man wants to know what religion we are. Shall I tell him DEMMYCRAT or 'PUBLICAN?"

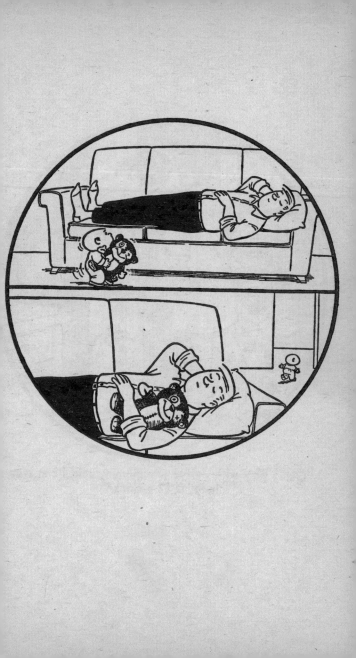

"Can I play with Jeffy? My mommy said I can stay here 'til 12 o'clock."

"I can't sit on THAT!"

"Oh, oh! I mailed my glove."

"Who am I being, Mommy? HO-HO-HO!"

"What's the zip code for the North Pole?"

"Mommy! Your door is stuck! It won't open!"

"That one'll be okay, Daddy. We can do like we always
and turn the scraggly side to the wall."

"Our Christmas cards are on the table
ready for you to mail."

"Look! Santa left the price on this!"

"I didn't even ASK for mittens, but I guess Santa knew
I needed them!"

"Okay, PJ, you can come in—but, DON'T TOUCH ANYTHING!"

"Could we go out today and buy something with the money
Grandma sent us?"

"While I'm at school, Mommy, will you keep an eye on my
things and don't let ANYBODY touch 'em?"

"Mommy! Jeffy used one of the clean towels instead of the
dirty one in the cabinet!"

"I'll take off the Donald Duck bracelet in the car.
It's the one Billy gave me for Christmas."